GW00642661

PORTRAIT OF
The QUANTOCK HILLS

CRAIG HUTCHINGS

HALSGROVE

First published in Great Britain in 2009

Copyright words and pictures © Craig Hutchings
This book has been part funded by a Sustainable Development Fund Grant
from the Quantock Hills AONB Service

All rights reserved. No part of this publication may be reproduced,
stored in a retrieval system, or transmitted in any form or by any
means without the prior permission of the copyright holder.

British Library Cataloguing-in-Publication Data
A CIP record for this title is available from the British Library

The author's royalties from the first print run are to be donated to the 'Friends of Quantock' charity

ISBN 978 1 84114 933 2

HALSGROVE
Halsgrove House,
Ryelands Industrial Estate,
Bagley Road, Wellington, Somerset TA21 9PZ
Tel: 01823 653777   Fax: 01823 216796
email: sales@halsgrove.com

Part of the Halsgrove group of companies
Information on all Halsgrove titles is available at: www.halsgrove.com

Printed and bound by Grafiche Flaminia, Italy

Craig's Acknowledgements

This book is dedicated with all my love, to my beautiful wife Bev and our daughters Amberley and Emily, who have had to endure endless nights of broken sleep with countless 4am alarm calls, in order for me to 'catch the light'.

A special thanks goes to my Father Ron, who gave me my first 35mm camera back in the 1970s, and from where my love of photography came.

And thanks to all my friends and family. In no particular order: John 'Big Bird' Hinchliffe, Helen, Calvin Flynn, Kerry – Diesel!, Al 'Pikey' Pike (Come on' Bath), Vicky 'vic-my-ster' Meaden, Ritchie Cook (Fred), Bob Mason, The lift share – Taff D, Mad George and his lordship John C, Julian Hull, Roy & Val, Mum, Neil, Keith & Karen, John & Lynn, Martin Wells, Mike 'the rut' Acreman, and all my friends on the Chinook & Puma IPTs.

LOCATION MAP – The Quantock Hills

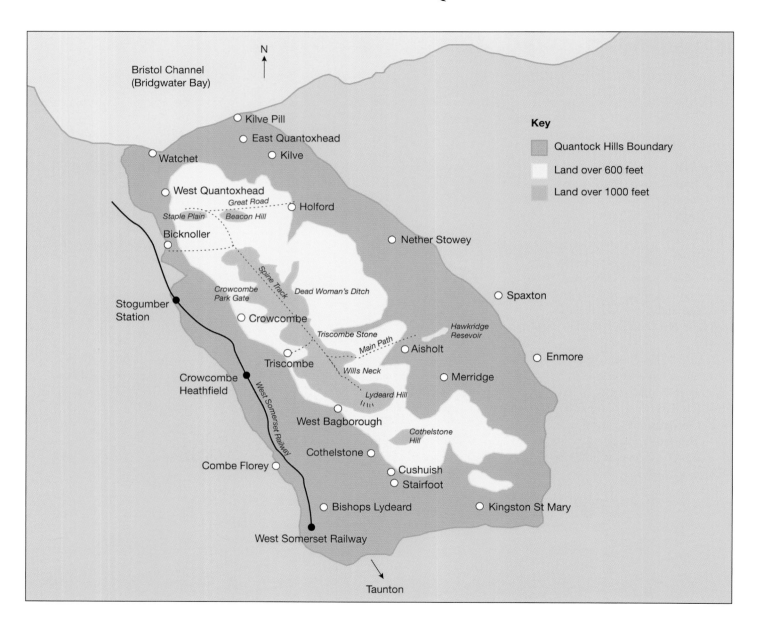

N

Bristol Channel
(Bridgwater Bay)

○ Kilve Pill

○ East Quantoxhead

○ Watchet   ○ Kilve

○ West Quantoxhead
                Great Road
Staple Plain   *Beacon Hill*   ○ Holford
Bicknoller
○

                              ○ Nether Stowey

Spine Track

Crowcombe   *Dead Woman's Ditch*
Park Gate

Stogumber   ○ Spaxton
Station
         ○ Crowcombe

                         Triscombe Stone   *Hawkridge*
                                              Resevoir
                              Main Path
         ○ Triscombe   ○ Aisholt   ○ Enmore
Crowcombe
Heathfield   *Wills Neck*
                                    ○ Merridge
                         Lydeard Hill

West Somerset Railway
                    ○ West Bagborough
                                    Cothelstone
                                    Hill
         ○ Cothelstone
Combe Florey ○
                         ○ Cushuish
                         ○ Stairfoot
              ○ Bishops Lydeard   ○ Kingston St Mary
West Somerset Railway

Taunton

Key

■ Quantock Hills Boundary

□ Land over 600 feet

■ Land over 1000 feet

Foreword

The Quantock Hills sit in one of England's finest counties, Somerset, and are probably one of this country's best kept secrets nestling in against their larger cousin Exmoor. But the Quantocks are so much more than a 'little Exmoor'. This gentle ridge of uplands rises from just a few feet above sea-level at Taunton and climbs to 1260 ft at Wills Neck, before dipping its shoulders in to the Bristol Channel, a mere 12 miles later. Size for size, in these few miles that make up the Quantocks, there can surely be a no more beautiful place in Britain. Indeed Coleridge and Wordsworth captured their simple beauty in verse and in doing so, wrote some of this country's most celebrated literature while staying in the hills in the 1790s. In his 'Recollections of Love' Samuel Taylor Coleridge, years after leaving West Somerset, was still enchanted with their charm.

> Eight springs have flown, since I last lay
> On sea-ward's Quantocks heathy hills,
> Where quiet sounds from hidden rills
> Float hear and there, like things astray,
> And high o'er head the sky-lark shrills.

Indeed, little has changed since those heady days of the romantic poets. So little wonder, with all the wonderful facets the hills have to offer, the open moorland, Jurassic coastline, charismatic farmland and magnificent woodland, the Quantocks were awarded in 1956, the distinction of being England's first Area of Outstanding Natural Beauty (AONB) and, furthermore, the Quantock Common (the open moorland) is designated as a Site of Special Scientific Interest (SSI). This serves to offer protection to this special landscape, which contains habitat of international importance.

My Welsh father-in-law, Roy, accompanied me on an early morning walk and commented as we sat down to enjoy a cup of coffee on Hurly Beacon. Surveying the all-encompassing panorama before us, he said with great conviction in his voice 'One hell of a backyard you've got here'. And indeed it is, ONE STUNNING BACKYARD!

Craig 'Hutch' Hutchings

East Quantoxhead
With the high tide lapping at the foot of the cliffs the sun breaks through a leaden sky to produce a fine end to the evening.

Seven Sisters

These magnificent beech trees keep an ever-present vigil over the Vale of Taunton Deane. Set high on the summit at Cothelstone Hill, they are subject to the worst the mighty south-westerly winds can throw at them during the winter months. So, almost inevitably, seven have become four, have become three over the years. However these handsome trees still manage to dominate the skyline in southern reaches of the hills.

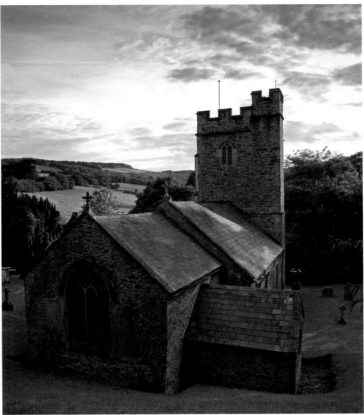

Aisholt
Set deep within the rolling countryside, beautiful evening light bathes Aisholt church in an almost chocolate box setting.

Left:
Woolston Moor
The West Somerset Railway is Britain's longest preserved line, and the section from Bishops Lydeard to Williton is regarded as one of England's most picturesque. This is perfectly demonstrated here as GWR Prairie Tank 5542, which spent most of its working life working Somerset's branch lines out of Taunton, re-enacts a scene from the 1940s, as the line cuts across Woolston Moor with the rain threatening to engulf Weacombe Hill in the distance.

Aisholt
Looking back towards the village of Aisholt as the sun breaks through the gloom, the rolling West-Somerset countryside as viewed from the common of the same name.

Left:
Aisholt Common
Nestling in next to Wills Neck, Aisholt Common is a real haven for wildlife, although these days, it appears to be becoming over-run with bracken.

Bagborough Plantation
Like no other native tree, the beech really does ooze the beautiful hues of autumn, especially when back-lit, like here at Bagborough Plantation

Bincombe
Early November and the golden leaves of the beech trees are thinning, letting the late autumn sunshine illuminate the forest floor.

Birches Corner
Birches Corner leads to one of the main car parks on the Quantocks, at Lydeard Hill. Set on the grass island, is one of the magnificent 'Somerset Finger' posts that are arguably the most aesthetically pleasing in the country. All the finger posts within the Quantocks have been beautifully restored with location collars with help from the AONB service.

Right:
Black Hill
The Quantocks are a walkers' and mountain bikers' paradise. You can almost hear the crunch of walking boots against the loose stones lying on the footpath, in this iconic view from Black Hill.

Hinkley Point

Although not strictly on the Quantocks, from wherever you look on the high ridge of the hills, your eyes are drawn inexorably to the haunting structure of the nuclear power station on the coast at Bridgwater Bay, which dominates the views looking north east towards the Bristol Channel.

Queen of the Wood

If the mighty oak is the king of the wood, then the beech is definitely the queen. There are many fine examples on the hills and indeed the Quantocks are well blessed with beautiful beech trees. This fine example is in the woods on Broomfield Hill.

Buzzards

Many ornithologists refer to this magnificent bird as the 'Englishman's Eagle' and it's not hard from this shot to see why, as this buzzard flies from an oak tree near Stairfoot. Is there any finer sight on a summer's afternoon, than a pair of buzzards circling on a thermal, taking them higher and higher? It is little wonder that the official emblem of the Quantocks is a buzzard, as the skies appear at times to be awash with these beautiful raptors.

Right:
A buzzard soaring the airways,
again near Stairfoot.

A buzzard in the field at Stairfoot

Cairns

These ancient cairns are dotted all over the hills. Their original purpose is unclear, but they are usually sited in a location with a fine view. As dawn breaks at Hare Knap, the first rays of sun illuminate the cairn as a fantastic vista of the Quantocks stretches out before it.

Above, top: Woodlands Hill. As the sun comes up over the Bristol Channel the cairn dominates the foreground. *Above, bottom:* Knackers Hole. With the imposing Dowsborough Hill Fort in the distance, this scene evokes a time we can only wonder about.

Cothelstone Manor
The impressive entrance to Cothelstone Manor. It's hard to imagine that in times past, this was where
Judge Jeffries hanged two Monmouth rebels, on the outer arches to deter other would-be insurgents.

Cothelstone Hill
The first major hill to rise out of the foothills to the north of Taunton.
A violent storm has just past, to leave the light dancing in and out of the showers.

Cothelstone Cottages and Church
Wisteria-dripped cottages with Cothelstone church in the background, a picture-postcard scene, quintessential England, right in the very heart of the Quantocks.

Crowcombe

The sun rises over one of the most delightful places on the Quantocks, sheltering as it does beneath the splendour of the high ridge.
This seemingly ageless village, set in the very heart of the hills, bisects the range wonderfully. To the north of the combe, lie the
heather-clad moorlands such as Hurley Beacon and Somerton. To the south, lies the great Quantock forest.
In the foothills, to the west of the great combe, lies wonderfully appealing farmland.

Crowcombe Park Gate
The starting point for all manner of folk to explore the hills,
from walkers to riders and cyclists alike. Crowcombe Park Gate sits high
on the open hillside and neatly marks their mid-point. The pull-in
just off the main road, can become a real bottleneck at the weekends,
as it seems half the county tries to park up.

Right:
Sunrise over Hare Knap
A glorious start to the day, as the sun, still beneath the horizon,
lights the high clouds in the sky.

Dead Woman's Ditch
A pony standing in the Iron Age linear earthwork known as Dead Woman's Ditch. However the name
is reputed to date only from 1789 when John Walford murdered his wife and left her body lying in the ditch.

Dog Pound Lane

Magnificent beech trees make a splendid avenue as you rise from Holford. The lane takes its name from the
dog pound at Holford from which it starts. In fact this lane is The Great Road (track) which runs from
Holford over Longstone Hill and Beacon Hill before finishing at Staple Plain.

Doniford Stream

Although blessed with many wonderful babbling brooks cascading down the various combes, the Quantocks are in fact devoid of a major watercourse such as the Exe or Barle on Exmoor. The closest the Quantocks get to a river is the wonderful Doniford Stream, looking the part after the winter rains have swollen the waters.

Dowsborough Hill Fort
The impressive Iron Age Dowsborough Hill Fort. This defensive earthwork covers 7 acres, much under scrub oak.

Drovers Road
Flanked by a beech hedge which has been allowed to grow up, this part of the road lies between Crowcombe Park Gate and Triscombe Stone. This track in fact runs the entire length of the hills, from Lydeard Hill in the south all the way to West Hill in the north.

Exmoor Ponies
Not looking out of place, Cothelstone Hill is the home to a fine herd of pure-bred Exmoor ponies.
Although wild-roaming ponies can be seen all over the Quantocks, these are the only 'Exmoors' on the hills.

Fallen Beech
Beech trees are notorious for falling, the average age of a beech probably being only 300 years.
Coupled with their shallow root system, a lot of trees on the Quantocks are now at the mercy of high winds.

Fennington
Drinker's delight, a field of barley, perhaps to be turned into a pint or two of ale,
stands in the evening light as showers bubble up over the higher ground.

Flaxpool

Two faces of the Quantocks side by side here at Flaxpool, the rich fertile farmland
overlooked by the mighty Wills Neck on a bright late summer's morning.

Frozen Heather
The common land and wild tops of the Quantocks are covered with a blanket of heather and bracken.
Here, an overnight frost has turned them into a shivering skeleton.

Halsway Manor
On the western slopes of the high ridge, Halsway is a Grade 2 listed building and is a wonderful example of a Somerset manor house. Today, it is the home of The Halsway Manor Society, the only residential folk centre in the country for traditional music, dance, and song.

Left:
Great Wood
Early morning mists dance through Great Wood to leave the forestry plantation an eerie haunted place.

Halsway Post
At Bicknoller and here at Halsway, the old oak posts were reinstated in 2008.
With the rain falling and the hill mist setting in, you can see why these posts
were once an important marker for the road across the top of the hills.

Right:
Hare Knap
The open moorland at dawn is a wonderful place when bathed with gentle
light. This time of morning on the open ground is when red deer may
often be sighted, taking an early morning breakfast before
being pushed down into the combes by walkers.

Hawkridge Reservoir
On a perfectly calm frosty morning, it's hard to imagine, this sheet of water not to have been here forever. But it is a relatively new addition to the Quantock landscape being constructed in the 1960s .

Sunrise, Hawsway
A feature of the Quantocks is the fine beech hedges, marking out fields and making a perfect frame on a day when the sun paints the sky red for a good 180 degrees, while mists dance around the vale below the high ridge.

Red Deer Hinds

The hinds are a welcome sight all over the hilltops and are often seen by walkers. *Top:* This one takes a well-earned sit-down in the fields around Alfoxton, where she has struck up a nice working relationship with this crow. The crow gets an easy meal by eating ticks on the deer's coat while the hind gets a free grooming. *Bottom:* The second hind is nicely illuminated on Black Ball Hill.

Hurley Beacon
Keeping an ever-present vigil over the hills, Hurley Beacon is only ever lit on special occasions now, such as Royal Jubilees.
These ancient beacons once served as bygone lookout points, warning of marauding invaders from the southwest approaches.

Kilve Pill
The tide retreats as great pools of water are left in the rocks ready for the sun to paint
a wonderful kaleidoscope on them.

Lady's Edge

One of the delights of the hills is the fan of combes running into Holford from the high ground. All the combes have wonderful babbling brooks winding their way off the hills. Here at Lady's Edge, on a grey but perfectly still day, the stream slows as it widens before joining another watercourse at Short Combe.

Hare Knap and Woodlands Hill
On an almost perfect autumn morning, with the sun winning the battle to burn off the high clouds,
the heavy fog lifts to reveal Hare Knap in the foreground and Woodlands Hill in the distance.

Lydeard Hill

A favourite stamping ground for the people of the large towns to the south of the hills, Taunton and Bridgwater. It's not hard to see why. What better way to unwind from the hustle and bustle of modern living, than with a bracing walk over a little piece of wilderness not more than 20 minutes from town.

Middle Hill
On a typically wet day, the tops of the hills are shrouded in mist. As the name suggests,
this is the middle hill of a series of three, sitting in between Lydeard Hill and Wills Neck.

Left:
Marrow Hill
Looking towards Marrow Hill and Great Hill from the very edge of the old Triscombe quarry workings.
A dreary overcast late summer's evening is broken by an almost blinding ray of light from the low sun.

Lydeard Hill Thorn
On a late spring morning, a thorn in full bloom stands on Lydeard Hill. Aisholt Common, in the distance,
is shrouded in unseasonable mist usually associated with autumn.

Moon Set
Sheep graze on a cold winter's afternoon, as the moon, magnified by a long lens and
its low angle in the sky, sets in behind two lone trees on Dene Hill Brake.

Parkend
A lone bluebell picked out against a sea of blue at Parkend.

Left:
Is there a finer sight in late spring than a carpet of bluebells on the wood
floor? Here at Parkend, they are beautifully backlit by the late afternoon sun.

Pheasant
With the number of shoots in and around the Quantocks, the
hills are blessed with large numbers of fantastically coloured birds.
Although not a native of these lands, the winter landscape in particular
wouldn't be the same without them. This cock bird stands in
his full glory in the fields by Cothelstone.

Right:
Quantock Vale
On a rain-sodden afternoon looking from the high ridge to the west,
the vale is suddenly lit with an almost biblical shaft of light to
illuminate the piece of land that lies in-between the main
ridge of the Quantocks and the Brendon Hills.

Roaring Stag
As on Exmoor, red deer are arguably the jewel in the crown of
the Quantocks. Is there a finer sight or sound in British Natural History
than a big 'Autumn Stag' roaring and strutting his stuff in an attempt
to round up some hinds to mate with? Here, this stag is roaring at
Foxes' Bottom near Aisholt Common.

Left:
Atlantic Depression
A perfect sunrise over Black Hill is engulfed, as a huge
depression sweeps up the Bristol Channel from the Atlantic.
Far below, Bridgwater Bay is about to become its latest victim
as the rain falls from its clouds.

Robin Upright's Hill
Late August heather makes a fine foreground as the sun rises over the fantastically named and misty Robin Upright's Hill.

Roe Deer

Alongside the red, the extremely shy roe deer is the other major deer species living on the Quantocks, mainly on farmland. This doe stands in a field of winter barley caught by a heavy frost near Stairfoot.

Royal Stag

A 12 point red deer stag is known as a 'Royal'. Although red deer are numerous on the hills, a mature animal such as this is quite rare. Here he stands on the side of Slaughterhouse Combe during the October rut.

Beacon Hill
Beacon Hill in the north west has fantastic views over the Bristol Channel and beyond to Wales.
Indeed on a clear day Pen-y-Fan, the highest mountain in Southern Britain, can be seen on the Brecon Beacons.
Here a lonesome sheep guards the view looking towards Minehead and Exmoor.

Mist, Short Combe
On a glorious day, Hare Knap on the left, raises its shoulders out of the
cold morning mist that has settled into Short Combe overnight.

Slaughterhouse Combe
Flanked by Black Ball Hill to the left, Somerton to the right and with Longstone Hill in the distance, the sun rises over Holford and cold morning air settles into one of the Quantocks' great combes at dawn. The complex of combes which wind their way down from the high ground into Holford – Slaughterhouse and Somerton feeding into Hodder, Frog and Lady running into Holford Combe – are without doubt the most spectacular on the Quantocks.

Snow on Middle Hill
With the Somerset Levels free from an overnight fall of snow, the golden
rays of the morning sun turn the Quantocks into a winter wonderland.

Snowdrops

The first of the year's wild flowers to show itself in February is the snowdrop. These hardy little plants are in abundance around the lanes and tracks in the southern foothills near Broomfield and here at Cushuish; they remind us that we have turned winter's corner and the promise of spring is soon to come.

Spring Beech

The woods at Bagborough come to life, as the warmer spring days bring the beech, with its gentle green shade, into leaf.

Spring Stag
A young red deer stag probably in its second or third year, makes
its way up onto the crown of the hills from Hawsway. Known
locally as a 'Springer', this youngster should in a few years time,
become one of the great autumn stags which roam the hills

Stag and Hind
Out on the open moorland at Somerton, this autumn
stag stands proudly with his hind during October. You
can see his left-hand antler has a kink in it. This is
where he probably bumped it earlier in the summer
when the antler was growing and still soft.

Stairfoot

If ever a name summed up its location then surely Stairfoot is it. For indeed it sits at the foot of the stairs leading up to the high ground with the footpath passing the new chic crop, Elephant Grass.

Stert Combe

Situated out on the open moorland, a good place to listen to the large stags roaring at each other during the October rut. From Bicknoller Post back towards Crowcombe Park Gate, the combes vibrate to the sound of bellowing stags.

Thorn

Ancient old thorns, like this one overlooking the Bristol Channel at the head of Smith's Combe, are among some of the oldest living things on the hills, with ages reaching maybe 700 years or more. Indeed, William Wordsworth so noted on one of his famous walks with Coleridge over the hills. Who knows, this thorn may have been the inspiration for the poem; it would have certainly been around.

There is a thorn; it looks so old,
In truth you'd find it hard to say,
How it could ever have been young,
It looks so old and grey.
Not higher than a two years' child
It stands erect this aged thorn;
No leaves it has, no thorny points;
It is a mass of knotted joints,
A wretched thing forlorn.
It stands erect, and like a stone
With lichens it is overgrown.

W. Wordsworth: 1798

Toulton

With Wellington monument standing on top of the Blackdown Hills on the other side of the Vale of Taunton Deane,
a gentle mist settles in the low land in-between these two great Somerset hill ranges.

Track at Frog Hill
Great walks can be had over the tops of the hills. Here a footpath passes
Frog Hill on an unseasonably warm winter morning.

Trig Point
The Ordnance Survey's trig point on Beacon Hill watches the sun rise up over the Bristol Channel.

Triscombe
A once important crossroads on the hills sitting in-between Wills Neck and Great Hill, is marked by the Bronze Age Triscombe Stone. Here the sun is setting behind a lone tree with the Brendon Hills in the distance.

Triscombe Stone
Once this fine artifact from the distant past stood proudly out in the open for travellers to find their bearings. Today however, it looks rather forlorn sitting in amongst the beach hedgerow that has sadly been allowed to grow up around it.

View from Wills Neck

The piercing summer's sun rising over Aisholt. Fantastic 360 degree views can be had from here: on a clear day, Exmoor, Wales, the Somerset Levels and Bristol Channel can all be viewed. As with all high ground though, it is often shrouded in low cloud and mist during the winter months and in the summer, a mixture of heat haze and pollution can often lead to disappointing results.

Vinny Combe

At times during the late spring Vinny Combe almost resembles the Himalayas as the whole combe is covered in rhododendrons. Without doubt in early June the place is awash with colour and scent as these invasive plants transform Vinny Combe. With this beauty there is however a down side. These plants smother all the native flora and there is a danger they could end up on the open moorland. To this end, they need to be kept in check and the big challenge is to keep the rhododendrons confined to the combe.

Sunrise Thorn
A sunrise against a twisted old thorn sitting high out on the moorland.

Watchet Harbour

Watchet oozes history. This is the place
where Samuel Taylor Coleridge supposedly got
the inspiration to write the poem 'Rime of the
Ancient Mariner' while staying at Nether Stowey.
The fair breeze blew, the white foam flew,
The furrow followed free ;
We were the first that ever burst
Into that silent sea.
Water, water, every where,
And all the boards did shrink ;
Water, water, every where,
Nor any drop to drink.
S.T. Coleridge: 1797

Above: The harbour at dawn, all still now
as Watchet no longer trades as a port.
Right: Half of the old harbour has now been
turned into a marina. Dawn, as the small
boats rest, awaiting their next trip out.

Above:
Watchet Beach
Watchet beach with the imposing West Hill in the distance.

Right:
Wilmot's Pool
The still morning air on a breathless day, turns the water in Wilmot's Pool into a mirror reflecting beautifully the dawn sky. Situated out on the high moor, this man-made dewpond was originally dug a few hundred years ago as a drinking hole for the stock put out on the hills. Today as well as the sheep and ponies it's also a favorite stopping-off point for wildlife.

Crowcombe Court

Crowcombe Court, a Grade 1 listed building, built between 1723–1739. It was described by Nikolaus Pevsner in *The Buildings of England* as 'the finest house of its date in Somerset, south of Bath' and it's easy to see why, as the early morning light beautifully picks out the magnificent architecture.

Crowcombe Heathfeild Station

The Grade 2 listed station at Crowcombe Heathfield on the West Somerset Railway, is the very embodiment of the GWR's branch lines so famed for linking isolated west country villages with a touch of style. Film and TV crews have been flocking to this pretty Quantock station for years; from the Beatles' 'Hard Day's Night', to 'The Land Girls', Crowcombe Station has made a wonderful setting.

Misty Fields
Looking towards Stogumber in late summer. Gentle mists formed by the cooler air of September, often transform the lower levels of the hills into an artist's watercolour scene.

Rainbow
As a violent summer shower moves on, the evening sun comes out to produce a wonderful rainbow over a cut field of barley at Stairfoot.

Red Deer, Blue Sea

With the Welsh coastline a mere 15 miles away, the good folk of Cardiff, as they wake to a beautiful late summer's morning, are totally unaware a herd of red deer have come out of Smith's Combe to catch the early morning sun overlooking the principality.

Snow, Open Moorland

A tell-tale, tyre track indicates a lone mountain cyclist has ventured out with snow still threatening in the skies. A white blanket covers the northern hills transforming them into an almost wilderness-like form.

Fallen Leaves
The golden shed leaves of autumn are in abundance all
over the woodlands on the Quantocks. Here, trapped
leaves lie in the stream running through Hanford Combe.

Stream at Holford Combe
As the leaves are falling during the autumn, Holford Combe, along with all the other combes,
turns to wonderful russet tones. You can see why Americans call this most wonderful of seasons the 'Fall'.

Thorncombe Hill
A biting east wind blowing across the moors, is belied by the
warm hues of a winter's sunrise as the path leads to Black Hill and beyond.

Cockercombe
The sun breaks though the mist at Cockercombe to leave these fir trees silhouetted against the light.

Great Hill
With Wills Neck shrouded in low cloud, the first rays of the day illuminate an
incomplete cairn on the National Trust-owned Great Hill.

Vinny Combe
A sunny day in Vinny Combe.

Roebuck Crossing
GWR 14xx 0-4-2T no 1450 looks every bit the part in the evening light as she heads towards Roebuck Crossing on the West Somerset Railway with the last train of the day.

Bluebells at Buncombe
An unexpected delight in amongst the evergreens at Buncombe, a beautiful
glade of beech trees with an accompanying carpet of bluebells.

Broomfield Hill
With Seven Sisters visible on Cothelstone Hill in the distance, a showery evening on
Broomfield Hill is momentarily broken as the sun makes a brief appearance.

Sunrise Over West Hill

A lone tree stands before the most fantastic sunrise over West Hill. There is often confusion as to the location of West Hill; in-fact there are two 'West Hills'. One is a lovely meadow near Crowcombe Park Gate and the other is here, the most northerly hill before the Quantocks disappear into the Bristol Channel.

Dawn over Dowsborough
A thin line of cloud sits above the imposing Dowsborough as day breaks over the northern hill range.

Frozen Rocks
The first of the morning's sun hits the ice creating a wonderful pattern. The water, which runs over these rocks in the bottom of Sheppard's Combe, has frozen solid as a severe frost descended on the hills the previous night.

Small GWR Prairie Tank 4561
Making a stirring sight as she climbs the bank to Stogumber on the West Somerset Railway on a January morning.

Kilve Beach
Situated at Kilve, these huge limestone pavements are one of the geological wonders of England, formed as countless high tides and Atlantic storms have pushed the cliffs back.

Harvested Fields
A classic English harvest scene at Cushuish, as the straw left by the combine
harvester leaves a reassuringly regimented pattern on the landscape.

Thorncombe Hill

A weak winter's sun rises over Black Hill and tries its best to warm a biting easterly wind
that has frozen a pool on Thorncombe Hill, on a January morning.

The Slades
Standing tall in the cold morning air, fir trees march backwards in silhouette. The Slades sit in the lower west corner of Great Wood abutting Aisholt Common and are laid down these days to a conifer plantation.

Moorland Bog

A bog out on the high moor. During periods of prolonged wet weather, the unsuspecting
walker can soon find his boots filling with water as he sinks knee high in mud!

Dawn on the Open Moor
The start of a new summer's day, skylarks are overhead singing their ever-present song and there is not
a breath of breeze in the air. The water in the pool makes a pleasing foreground for this moorland scene.

Somerton Combe
The flanks of the big northern combes are covered with scrub oak, making great cover for the wildlife as walkers and cyclists unwittingly push them off the open moorland.

Weacombe and Beyond
Looking from Thorncombe Hill across Weacombe and onto Minehead in the distance. On certain days when the atmospheric conditions are right, distant places can almost appear to be within touching distance rather than the huge distances they are.

Triscombe Quarry

Triscombe quarry is in shadow from the sun coming up from the east. Situated on the north-west flank of Wills Neck, the quarry has taken quite a chunk out of this handsome hill before closing in the 1990s.

Frog Hill
A thorn is silhouetted against the mid morning's sun on Frog Hill looking across to Dowsbrough and Robin Upright's Hill.

Beech in Autumn
With blue skies prevailing on a warm autumn afternoon, the beech woodlands
in and around the Quantocks are a real picture with their changing colours.

Blizzard Conditions
With the snow still swirling in the high winds, Dibbles Elbow is transformed with Siberianesque conditions as the sun comes up.

5am Beacon Hill
On a perfect summer's morning with the sun rising over the northern range and with 16 hours of daylight to follow, what better than to follow the track from the furthest point north all the way back to Stairfoot in the foothills in the south.

Buncombe/Broomfield
Where Buncombe merges with Broomfield a gentle mist hangs to the fields on a still summer's morning.

Below:
Broomfield
Taunton way below is shrouded in fog as round bales waiting to be collected sit on what is the highest agricultural land on the hills.

Merridge

The classic patchwork farmland around Merridge on a perfect start to a blistering hot summer's morning, as gentle mists cling to the land before being burnt off.

Below:
Lane to Toulton

The hills are criss-crossed with these idyllic country lanes. You can almost hear a cuckoo in this shot as the lane makes its way to Toulton on an early summer's morning.

Lone Oak

Famed as the hills are for the magnificent beech trees held within its borders, there are some quite majestic oak trees doted around. This oak stands, like so many others, isolated in a field, here near Bishops Lydeard.

West Somerset Coast Path
The Quantock coastline forms a part of the West Somerset Coast Path. As the sun sets over
the Bristol Channel on a stormy evening, Blue Ben in the middle distance juts out into the bay.

Birch Tree in Bud
A birch tree bursting into life watches over the view of Middle Hill and Aisholt Common in the distance.
A seasonal indicator, the birch is usually the first to bud among the native trees.

Islands in the Mist
With the whole of Somerset
under a blanket of thick fog,
Great Hill and Cowcombe Park
raise their heads above the gloom
which lies below their summits
to be greeted by bright sun.

Below:
Dawn over Quantock Vale
A summer's dawn breaks over the
fertile vale looking towards the
southern part of the high ridge.

Snow at Stairfoot
The oak tree sitting in the field at Stairfoot, casts its shadow upon the snow.

Snow, Dene Hill Brake
With the wind whipping up a blizzard the previous evening, the snow has formed a perfect covering on the limbs of this tree on Dene Hill Brake.

Ball Lane
The lane is in fact a bridleway which takes you from the southern foothills at Stairfoot onto the crown of the hills at Cothelstone. An overnight fall of snow is followed by bright sun turning the track into a Christmas card scene.

115

Snowdrops, Cushuish Lane
Snowdrops pushing up past felled logs.

Cockercombe
The outline of Cokercombe is silhouetted against a stormy sunrise.

Attacking the Bank
A GWR 0-6-0 Collet Goods Engine,
turns the sky black as she makes an
assault on the bank to Crowcombe
Station with the first train of the
day from Bishops Lydeard, on the
West Somerset Railway.

Above:

Dead Tree

With Foxes' Bottom to the right, a dead tree sits in a small basin amongst the remnants of the previous summer's bracken on Aisholt Common.

Right:

Frozen Water

After a hard frost, the water in one of the many pools sitting in the tracks has frozen around some foliage leaving an intriguing pattern to catch the morning sun.

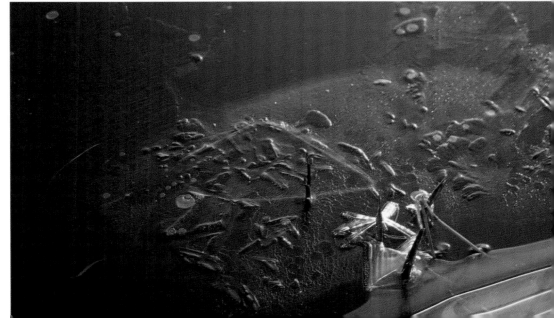

Cothelstone in Mist
The mist swirls around beautiful Cothelstone with the church and village sitting below its majestic hill.

Daybreak
With the lights around the coast still burning bright, the sun is still a good
30 minutes from rising as the Quantocks greet another day.

Combe Florey
Low bright sunlight washes out the definition of the farmland around Combe Florey.

West Bagborough
A tree stands proudly, looking out on the magnificent spectacle of atmospheric autumn mist sitting in the low ground, as the rising sun paints the morning clouds a delicate shade of orange.

Round Baling
These round bales, a relatively modern farming phenomenon, are aesthetically pleasing on a late summer's evening with the high range looking on.

Heather
The Purple Headed Mountain in the hymn 'All Things Bright And Beautiful' refers to Dunkery Beacon,
in another part of Somerset to the west on Exmoor. But equally the high peaks of the Quantocks are awash with the
colour in late August, and it's easy to see how the inspiration came to write the most famous of hymns.

Tetton
Sitting just above Kingston St Mary, the freshly harvested field looks down on
the Vale of Taunton Deane and the Blackdown Hills beyond.

Hawkridge Reservoir
Dawn breaks over the still waters.

Sheppard's Combe
Dawn over a delightful scene, depicting a vision a lot people will have of these silvan combes,
which are an integral part of the Quantock scene.

Kenely Bottom
A vapour trail is lit up as the sun rises up over Kenely Bottom. Left by a passing airliner, the passengers jetting off to far flung destinations are blissfully unaware, as the mist rises, of the unfolding beauty beneath them.

Below:
Wills Neck from Hurley Beacon
Looking back south from Hurley Beacon, you get a sense of how Wills Neck, the highest point of the hills, towers over the surrounding land.

Quantock Vale
A light mist hangs in the vale on a summer's morning.

Sunlit Trees
With the side of a combe still cast in shadow, a couple of trees are wonderfully picked out in a blaze of light from the sun.

Watchet at Twilight

A man called John Short, otherwise known as 'Yankee Jack', sailed from Watchet, breaking the blockades during the American Civil War. He sang for Cecil Sharp, 57 sea shanties of which 43 appear in Sharp's 'English Folk Shanties'.

Bluebells
Bluebells mixed in along with beech trees at 20 Acre Plantation, make for a heart-warming spring scene.

West Quantoxhead
With the Welsh coastline visible on a perfect May day, West Quantoxhead is bathed in glorious sunshine.

Beech in Autumn
On a warm autumn afternoon, the beech woodlands in and around the Quantocks are alive with dazzling colours.

Volis Hill
Outstanding views of Taunton are commanded by Volis Hill in the southernmost reaches of the Quantocks.

Paradise

The Quantocks are a vision of paradise to those who live and work in them, but the wood near Cothelstone is actually named Paradise. This however is a vision of paradise resembling Norway as the snow sits heavily on the branches of these fir trees.

Dawn
The first rays of the sun break over Luxborough.

Stream, Hodder's Combe
A stream tumbles down from the moorland above, babbling its way down Hodder's Combe on its way to Holford.

Bicknoller Post
Water sits in a puddle as the sun comes past Bicknoller Post.

7820 Dinmore Manor

Dinmore Manor awaits its turn of duty at Bishops Lydeard as the morning sun catches
the smoke rising from the copper-banded chimney on this GWR-designed engine.

Ponies in the Mist
A couple of ponies enjoying breakfast out on the open moorland.

Ammonite
The layered rock bed cliffs on the coast are rich in relics of life from prehistoric times.
Here a mighty ammonite, now heavily covered in lichens, sits perfectly in a wall at East Quantoxhead.

Stacked Timber
Covered in snow at 20 Acre Plantation.

Back-lit Beech

This magnificent beech tree lives alongside the main Bridgwater road running from Cothelstone to Buncombe. As if blessed by the Patron Saint of Travellers, St Christopher, the motorist gets a fantastic sight during October as the sun has swung sufficiently far south to backlight this beautiful tree, showing autumn in all its glory without even leaving the car!

Oak in the Mist

This mighty oak stands alongside the bridleway at 'Ball Lane', cutting a mighty fine silhouette as the sun breaks through heavy clouds to make waves in the mist.

War Memorial

Just off the Great Road (main track), half way up Longstone Hill from Holford, these fine fir trees were planted along with the
accompanying stone as a lasting memorial to the men and women of Holford and Kilve who served in the Second World War.
We are all reminded of the sacrifices others made for the freedom we all enjoy. If it wasn't for the 'brave few', none of
us could enjoy the beautiful countryside in Great Britain today.